OFF TO TAMIL NADU

SONIA MEHTA

PUFFIN BOOKS

An imprint of Penguin Random House

PUFFIN BOOKS

USA | Canada | UK | Ireland | Australia | New Zealand | India | South Africa | China | Singapore

Puffin Books is part of the Penguin Random House group of companies whose addresses can be found at global.penguinrandomhouse.com

Published by Penguin Random House India Pvt. Ltd
4th Floor, Capital Tower 1, MG Road,
Gurugram 122 002, Haryana, India

First published in Puffin Books by Penguin Random House India 2017

Text, design and illustrations copyright © Quadrum Solutions Pvt. Ltd 2017
Series copyright © Penguin Random House India 2017

Picture Credits

Title page/Covers: Gopurum (William Cushman/Shutterstock.com); P 11: Paddy fields (CRS PHOTO/Shutterstock.com); P 18: Street view of the French quarter, Puducherry (Yvdalmia/Shutterstock.com); P 30: Movie poster outside AVM Productions (Marco Saroldi/Shutterstock.com), Huge movie posters at the entrance of AVM Productions, Chennai (Marco Saroldi/Shutterstock.com); P 35: Women making rangoli (cornfield/ Shutterstock.com); P 36: Corridors of Ramanathaswamy Temple, Rameswaram, Tamil Nadu, India (CRS PHOTO/Shutterstock.com); P 38: Thanjavur (AJP/Shutterstock.com); P 40: Tractor with hay (Ailisa/Shutterstock.com), Workers working in the paddy field (Ailisa/Shutterstock. com); P 41: Workers in a tea estate (sixpixx/Shutterstock.com); P 60: Paddy fields (CRS PHOTO/Shutterstock.com)

The views and opinions expressed in this book are the author's own and the facts are as reported by her, which have been verified to the extent possible, and the publishers are not in any way liable for the same.

The information in this book is based on research from bonafide sites and published books and is true to the best of the author's knowledge at the time of going to print. Conversations have been created to enliven and narrate the story and are not verbatim utterances. The author is not liable for any further changes or development in incidents occurring post the publication of this book.

ISBN 9780143440758

Design and layout by Quadrum Solutions Pvt. Ltd

Printed at Repro India Limited

www.penguin.co.in

This is a legitimate digitally printed version of the book and therefore might not have certain extra finishing on the cover.

Hello Kids!

I'm so happy you are reading this book. India is an incredible country and there are lots of things about it that we never get to hear about.

I discovered India because my father was in the Indian army. He was posted to many places all over India—and we dutifully followed him. Can you imagine that by the time I was in the tenth standard, I had changed nine schools? Of course it was hard making new friends almost every year, but the good part was that I got to live in so many places. Right from Kerala, where I was born, to Kashmir, Jhansi, Shillong, Chandigarh, Goa . . . the list is long.

Every time I go to a new place, I feel amazed at how different each state is from the other—and yet, how similar. Did you know that we can see monuments from the Stone Age right here in India? Or that we have more than twenty official languages, and most Indians know three or four on an average? Or even that some of the world's most amazing scientific marvels were invented in India?

Oh, there are many, many, many fun and fantastic things about the states of India, which we simply must get to know.

So get your backpack ready, get set to meet some new friends and join me on a fun trip as we DISCOVER INDIA, STATE BY STATE.

I hope you enjoy reading this book as much as I have enjoyed writing it. I would love to hear from you. So do write to me at sonia.mehta@quadrumltd.com.

Lots of love,
Sonia Aunty

Mishki and Pushka have come to visit Earth from their home planet, Zoomba. They have never seen such an amazing place. Zoomba doesn't have trees and mountains and rivers like Earth does. But the people look exactly the same. When they come to Earth, they meet a sweet old man whom they call Daadu Dolma. Daadu Dolma shows them all the wonderful places in India and tells Mishki and Pushka all about them.

Mishki and Pushka can't believe what they see. They have seen a lot of Earth, but they have never, ever seen a place like India.

They are off to explore India state by state :)

Mishki

Mishki is a curious little girl. She is always asking loads of questions. On her home planet, she is always getting into trouble for poking her nose into things that are not her business.

Pushka

Pushka is Mishki's brother. He loves adventure. He is always ready to try a new challenge. Whether it's climbing a mountain, or diving into a cold, cold sea, he is up for it.

Daadu Dolma

Daadu Dolma is a wise old man who has lived on Earth longer than the mountains and seas. No one knows quite how old he is, but he certainly has been around. He knows everything about everything.

Mishki and Pushka are having a wonderful time discovering state after lovely state.

Their next stop is Tamil Nadu.

'I know how to speak Tamil,' boasts Pushka.

'Oh really! Then tell me how to say "hi" in Tamil?' asks Mishki disbelievingly.

'Vanakkam,' says Pushka triumphantly.

Daadu Dolma laughs. 'Quite right! Where did you learn that? But come now! It's time to go. We have much to see and know in Tamil Nadu. Are you all packed and ready?'

'YES!' shout Mishki and Pushka together. They are

OFF TO TAMIL NADU!!!

EDGE OF THE WATER

Tamil Nadu has a lovely location. It sticks out into the sea, but guess what! It has water from both the Bay of Bengal and the Indian Ocean lapping its shores. That's because the Indian Ocean is to its south and the Bay of Bengal is to its east. No wonder Tamil Nadu has wonderful beaches!

ON THE MAP

To see exactly where Tamil Nadu is on the map of India, go to http://www.mapsofindia. com/maps/india/india-political-map.htm

Karnataka

Andhra Pradesh

Kerala

Tamil Nadu

HAPPY NEIGHBOURS

Tamil Nadu has three happy neighbours. There are Andhra Pradesh and Karnataka sharing its northern border, and Kerala sitting prettily on the west. At its southern-most tip, like a lovely toe ring, is Kanyakumari. You may have heard people say 'From Kashmir to Kanyakumari.' What they mean is from the northern-most to the southern-most tip of India.

CITY CITY BANG BANG

Tamil Nadu has some really large cities. Chennai (which used to be called Madras) is the capital city. Other big cities you will hear of are Coimbatore, Madurai, Tiruchirapalli, Salem, Ooty (or Udhagamandalam), Kodaikanal and Rameshwaram. There are many, many big cities to visit.

The railway station at Chennai is magnificent.

THE LIFELINE OF TAMIL NADU

Do you know which river quenches Tamil Nadu's thirst? It's the Kaveri! It starts in the cool, green region of the Coorg in Karnataka and weaves its way all across Tamil Nadu. It creates a green and fertile delta, called the Thanjavur-Nagapattinam delta. (Try pronouncing that right: THAN-JA-VOOR NAGA-PATTI-NUM.) This is called the granary of Tamil Nadu because most of its grains are grown here. The other main rivers are the Palar, Pennar, Vaigai and Tamiraparani.

WHERE THE MOUNTAINS MEET

The Eastern and Western Ghats—both of which are mountain ranges—meet each other in Tamil Nadu. Because of these, a large part of Tamil Nadu is cool, green and beautiful.

Kaveri River

TROPICS, HERE WE COME!

You could say that Tamil Nadu has a tropical climate. This means that it is hot most of the year and wet during the monsoons. The people of Tamil Nadu sweat under the scorching sun in May and June, which are the hottest months. The sea breeze cools the land in December and January, and a mild winter sets in.

IT'S RAINING, IT'S POURING

The rainy season in Tamil Nadu is between October and December. The mountains and hilly regions—especially in the western part—get the most rain. The winds that bring rain to Tamil Nadu sweep in from the north-east. This rain is important for growing rice, which is an important crop in Tamil Nadu because everyone here just LOVES rice.

RHYME TIME

Pushka has become a poet. But he's stuck. He needs words that rhyme with RICE. Can you help him out?

R I C E

HOW CAN A MOUNTAIN BE BLUE?

The Nilgiri mountains are lovely mountains in the western part of Tamil Nadu. People say they got the name because of a beautiful blue flower called the Strobilanthes kunthiana that grows wild in the forests. Some others believe that it is because when you see the Nilgiri mountains from afar, they look blue.

Nilgiri means blue mountain.

The highest point of the Nilgiris is a place called Doddabetta. Oh wow, look at the view! Hundreds of people visit Doddabetta just for the beautiful view.

View from Doddabetta

MMM . . . WHAT'S THAT LOVELY SMELL?

The fragrant eucalyptus tree grows in plenty in the Nilgiri area. If you walk through the forests, you pick up the minty scent of eucalyptus. People make oil from this tree. This oil is good for reducing pain, for toothaches, and for coughs and colds.

CROPS AND CROPS

Tamil Nadu can be called an agricultural state too! There are vast paddy fields where farmers grow rice. In fact, rice is Tamil Nadu's favourite staple food, and almost every meal has some kind of rice. Farmers also grow lots of bananas, tapioca, natural rubber, coconut, groundnuts, coffee, tea and sugar cane.

CROP SHOP

In the word grid, find all the things that grow in Tamil Nadu.

S	U	G	A	R	C	A	N	E
J	L	R	F	I	O	T	E	A
R	J	O	P	C	F	Z	D	B
Y	F	U	E	E	F	G	C	V
P	X	N	F	G	E	W	E	H
Y	W	D	Q	W	E	T	C	W
B	A	N	A	N	A	P	V	A
R	P	U	W	S	E	D	F	Z
G	W	T	C	W	D	U	T	G
C	O	C	O	N	U	T	S	M

LET'S GO WILD 🐾

Can you imagine that there are more than 2000 species of wildlife in Tamil Nadu? As there are lots of forest areas, the government has protected them to keep wildlife safe. There are large mammals like elephants, leopards, tigers, gaurs, Nilgiri langurs, giant squirrels, sambar deer and sloth bears.

CHIRPY CHIRPY CHEEP CHEEP

Tamil Nadu has plenty of amazing birds too. Some live there, and some migrate there during certain seasons. There are birds like darters, herons, cormorants, openbill storks, grey pelicans, spoonbills—the list is long and you would have to go there to see these amazing creatures.

Darter

Openbill stork

Spoonbill

FISHY FISH

There are some fantastic sea creatures you can spot in the waters of Tamil Nadu. Dugongs, dolphins, turtles and lots of interesting types of fish can be seen here. Pushka wants to go deep sea diving. But not yet! There's a lot more for him to see.

FUN FACTS

State animal
Nilgiri Tahr

State bird
Emerald Dove

State tree
Palm Tree

State flower
Gloriosa superba

SPOT THEM ALL

Pushka is on the forest trail.

Find ten differences in the two pictures given here.

Long, long ago

Daadu Dolma, how come there are so many old looking temples all over the place?

That's because Tamil Nadu is a very, very, very old state. Thousands of years old, in fact.

THOUSANDS OF YEARS AGO

Around 1500 BCE, the Aryans, who were from different parts of Europe, attacked India from the Himalayas. A clan of people called the Dravidians, who lived in the north, moved to the south to get away from the wars and fights. They decided to find their own place to live. They reached the south of India and settled there, making them the original Tamilians. They called their new home Tamilham.

TRADING WITH THE WEST

Tamilham was wonderfully located for trade. The Tamilians began to establish trade with ancient Egypt, Greece and Rome. The land began to prosper. Soon, various royal dynasties in India began to fight for ownership of the land. Five main Hindu dynasties—the Cholas, Cheras, Pandyans, Pallavas and Chalukyas—ruled this land for different periods in time. Each of them brought their own special touch to the region.

Chola King

Pandyan King

Chera King

THE TEMPLE BUILDERS

First came the Cholas. They were powerful kings and even conquered a part of Ceylon (now called Sri Lanka). They built some of Tamil Nadu's most beautiful temples. Then came the Pallavas, who ruled for nearly 400 years. They brought their own style of architecture. Soon, they were overthrown by another Chola king, Rajaraja Chola and his son Rajendra Chola.

WHAT'S ODD?

In each of the rows, there's one word that is odd. Circle that.

TEMPLE	CHURCH	MOSQUE	SYNAGOGUE	MALL
EGYPT	GREECE	ITALY	ENGLAND	CHENNAI
CHOLAS	PANDYANS	PALLAVAS	CHALUKYAS	PORTUGUESE

FIGHTING FOR RULE

The Pallavas were knocking at the Chola door and soon overthrew them. But not for long. A Muslim king called Alauddin Khilji attacked the land and took over. His armies destroyed many cities, including Madurai. But the Hindu kings fought back and created a new empire called Vijaynagar. They built a beautiful capital city called Hampi, which is in today's Karnataka.

MUSLIM INVASION

Many Muslim rulers fought for this rich and wonderful land. Hyder Ali and his son, the famous Tipu Sultan, ruled for a while. But, by this time, the British had made an appearance. Tipu Sultan fought many battles with the British before losing and giving up.

Alauddin Khilji

HERE COME THE WESTERNERS

The Western world, particularly the Dutch and French, wanted to trade with India through Tamilham. They began to set up colonies. But, by this time, the British had already taken over the rest of India. Now, there were battles between the British, Dutch and French. Soon, the British drove away the Dutch. But the French held on tightly to their colony, Puducherry (earlier known as Pondicherry.)

If you visit Puducherry, you will feel as though you are in France. People speak French, serve French food and have a different way of life from the rest of Tamil Nadu.

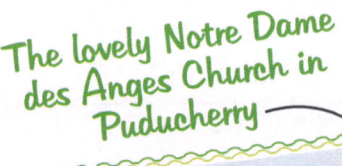
The lovely Notre Dame des Anges Church in Puducherry

Street view of the French quarter in Puducherry

WE WANT TO BE FREE

Along with the rest of India, people in Tamilham (by now it was called Madras Presidency) began to fight the British. They too wanted to be independent. When the British finally left and India became independent, Madras Presidency became Madras State. But did you know this? It not only included today's Tamil Nadu but also parts of Andhra Pradesh and Kerala.

Did you know?
There was a man known as Veerapandiya Kattabomman, who was a brave freedom fighter from Tamil Nadu. He fought long and hard against the British to help India become free. In 1999, a stamp was issued in his honour.

THE LANGUAGE DIVIDE

The people of Andhra Pradesh and Kerala spoke different languages. Finally, in 1968, based on language, the state of Madras was renamed Tamil Nadu. It included only Tamil-speaking people.

People in Andhra Pradesh speak Telugu.

People in Kerala speak Malayalam.

People in Tamil Nadu speak Tamil.

View of a valley in Kodaikanal

HILL STATIONS

During the time that the British occupied India, they found the heat of Madras hard to bear. They went looking for the cold, wet climate of England and found it in the Nilgiri mountains. They built small cities that looked and felt like their cities back home in England. Hill stations like Ooty and Kodaikanal have British street names to this day. The houses and buildings are in the British style too.

CRACK THE CODE

See what each letter stands for. Replace it in the blanks. And you will get the answer of what the Indians were trying to tell the British.

W = 1   E = 2   A = 3   N = 4   T = 5   O = 6

B = 7   F = 8   R = 9

1 2   1 3 4 5   5 6   7 2   8 9 2 2

___ ___   ___ ___ ___ ___   ___ ___   ___ ___   ___ ___ ___ ___ .

Talk time

Hey, let's meet some Tamil people and talk to them in their language.

But first we have to know something more than just hello, silly.

Come on, then. Let's practise some common words and phrases. But Tamil has some long words, so you must try and pronounce them carefully.

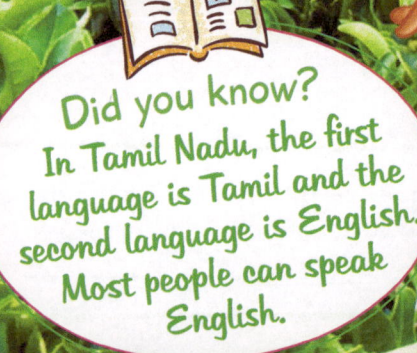

Did you know?
In Tamil Nadu, the first language is Tamil and the second language is English. Most people can speak English.

Hi! = Vanakkam!

What's your name?
= Unga pérenna?

My name is Mishki.
= En péru Mishki.

I/You = Naan/
Neenga

Big = Periya

Small = Chinna

Happy birthday!
= Pirandha naal
vazhthukkal!

Thank you.
= Romba nandri.

Sorry!
= Mannikkanum!

Good night!
= Iravu vanakkam!

Good bye!
= Poittu varén!

MATCH THE WORDS

Pushka is practising his Tamil. Help him by matching the Tamil words to their meanings.

| Hi | Sorry | Happy birthday! | Good night! | You! | What's your name? |

| Iravu vanakkam! | Neenga! | Mannikkanum | Unga pérenna? | Pirandha naal vazhthukkal!! | Vanakkam |

A peep into their life

Daadu, what are all those colourful buildings with statues on them?

Those are temples. Inside them are statues of Tamil Nadu's many, many Gods. Tamil Nadu has thousands of temples—both big and small. That's because most Tamil people are religious.

MANY RELIGIONS

Tamil Nadu has a mix of religions. The largest number of people are Hindus. There are many Christians, Jains and Muslims too! There are colourful temples, mosques and churches dotted all around Tamil Nadu. In villages, families have their own temples. Almost every home has a prayer room. Isn't that nice?

The people of Tamil Nadu pray to several gods, and some of these are called 'guardian gods' of different villages.

MURUGAN

Murugan is a much-loved god, who has been worshipped for thousands of years.

MARIAMMAN

Mariamman is an ancient goddess, who was worshipped even before the Dravidians were pushed to the south by the Aryans.

KARRUPASWAMY

Karrupaswamy is a guardian god, who people believe will protect them from all evil.

AYYANNAR

Ayyannar is yet another guardian god of villages. There are statues of him on the outskirts of many villages. There is always a figure of a horse with him, for people believe he rides around on the horse to patrol the village and keep it safe.

WRITE ON!

Tamil literature is probably the oldest in India. In those days, as far back as the third century BCE, people wrote on stone. While most of it was in the form of religious poetry, long stories were written about love and kings too. Some centuries later, people began writing songs and hymns in honour of saints. A famous poet called Kamban, during the Chola rule, wrote the 'Kamba Ramayana'—one of Tamil's most important works of literature.

Kamban, the famous Tamil poet

SUCH OLD MUSIC

Tamil Nadu shares a rich tradition of music with its neighbours. Hundreds of years ago, the people of south India developed Carnatic music, one of the oldest forms of music in the world. It is as much a science as it is an art. Most of the songs are devoted to gods or saints.

FAMOUS CARNATIC SINGERS

Purandara Dasa is considered the father of Carnatic music. Tyagaraja, Muthuswami Dikshitar and Shyama Shastri are three other famous Carnatic musicians who have composed thousands of songs that people love and listen to even today.

Purandara Dasa

Tyagaraja

Muthuswami Dikshitar

Shyama Shastri

THE BEAT AND THE TUNE

Musical instruments play an important part in Carnatic music. Here are some important ones.

MRIDANGAM

This is called the king of percussion. It is made from the wood of a jackfruit tree, with animal skin tightly attached to the two sides of a hollow wooden drum.

VEENA

The veena is a stringed instrument, which is usually made from a single piece of wood of the jackwood tree. There are many types of veenas, like the rudra veena, the vichitra veena and the Saraswati veena. The rudra veena was used occasionally in Carnatic music. But it isn't very popular any more.

Saraswati veena

Vichitra veena

Rudra veena

NADASWARAM

This is a wind instrument like the flute. It has finger holes that the musician uses to create different notes.

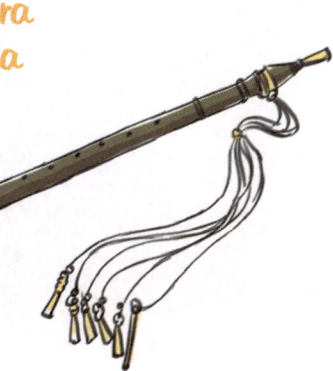

Classical dance is a really big deal in Tamil Nadu. Many girls and boys learn classical dance right from when they are little children. Then, when their teacher feels they are ready, they perform for the first time in front of an audience. This is a big event called the arangetram.

BHARAT NATYAM, DANCE FOR THE GODS

This dance is one of India's oldest. It used to be performed in temples and in the courts of kings. The women who danced for the gods in temples were called devdasis. They taught their daughters this dance, and so it went on for centuries. Soon, the devdasi system fell apart. Great dancers worked hard to take this dance form from the temples to the stage, where everyone could see it and enjoy it.

Now, there are thousands of schools all over the world where this dance is taught.

SNAKE DANCE

In Tamil culture, the snake is believed to be the protector of health and happiness. The snake dance is an amazing dance in which the dancers move with the same twists as snakes do. The dancers dress in tightly fitted clothes that look like the skin of a snake.

KARAGATTAM

This is a folk dance. The dancer balances a pot of water on her head. Villagers perform this dance to make the goddess of rain and goddess of rivers happy.

KOLATTAM

This is a fun dance. Only women perform this. They tap two sticks against each other, and this makes a sound. In another style, they hold colourful ropes that are tied to a tall pole. The women dance in a circle, weaving in and around each other, while the ropes make a patterned knot. What fun! But don't they all get tangled?

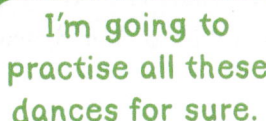

I'm going to practise all these dances for sure.

A FESTIVAL OF DANCE

The Natyanjali Festival is dedicated to Lord Nataraja. This god is known as the lord of dance. This festival is held in a place called Chidambaram and goes on for five days. During this time, people perform dances at the Nataraja temple.

A WEDDING OF THE GODS

The Chithirai Festival is held in the city of Madurai every year. People recreate the wedding ceremony of Princess Meenakshi (she was a princess of the Pandyan dynasty) and Lord Sundareswarar.

WALKING ON HOT COALS

The Kavadi Festival is the most exciting. People pray to Lord Muruga. They believe that the more you suffer, the more blessings you get. To show their devotion, each worshipper carries a stick on their shoulders. Two baskets that are filled with rice and milk hang on each end of this stick. Some devotees also walk on red-hot coals while carrying this. Such is the faith of the Kavadi bearers that people say they don't even feel the heat.

OUCH!

OUCH!

CELEBRATING HARVEST

Pongal is a harvest festival. People, especially farmers, celebrate this to thank the sun, the rain, the cattle and all of nature for helping them get a good harvest. In every home, people make a sweet dish of rice, jaggery and milk. Yummmm!

TAMING THE BULL

Jallikattu is an ancient sport. It is said that in the olden days, it was played to find a strong husband for a girl. An untamed bull would be left loose, and the man who managed to tame the bull by holding on to its horn would win the maiden. Over the years, it became a sport where people displayed their strength and bravery.

Now, it is played during the festival of Pongal. People ensure that no bulls are harmed during this sport.

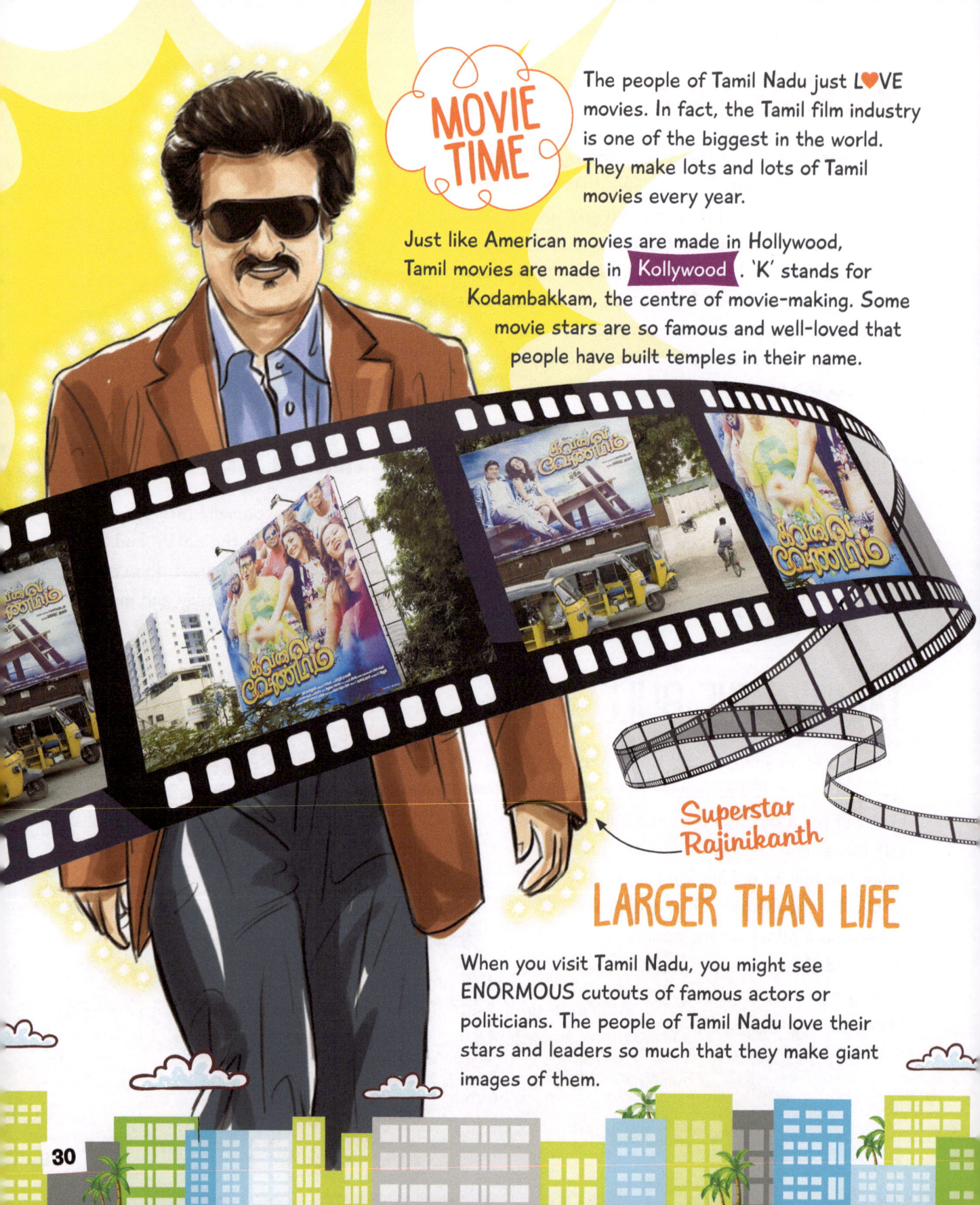

MOVIE TIME

The people of Tamil Nadu just L♥VE movies. In fact, the Tamil film industry is one of the biggest in the world. They make lots and lots of Tamil movies every year.

Just like American movies are made in Hollywood, Tamil movies are made in Kollywood. 'K' stands for Kodambakkam, the centre of movie-making. Some movie stars are so famous and well-loved that people have built temples in their name.

Superstar Rajinikanth

LARGER THAN LIFE

When you visit Tamil Nadu, you might see ENORMOUS cutouts of famous actors or politicians. The people of Tamil Nadu love their stars and leaders so much that they make giant images of them.

CROSSWORD TIME

Pushka wants to cross-check all that he has learnt. Help him crack the clues.

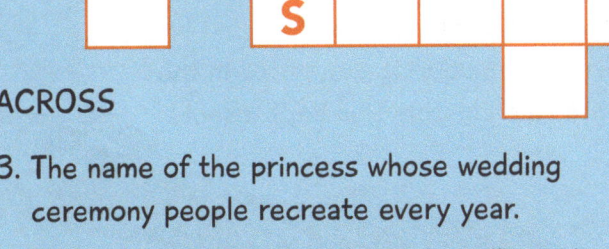

The crossword grid contains the following starting letters:
1. N
2. R
3. M
4. H
5. R
6. D
7. K
8. P
9. B
10. N
11. C
12. S

ACROSS

3. The name of the princess whose wedding ceremony people recreate every year.

5. The colour of coals when people walk on them.

8. The festival to thank nature.

11. The hot material people walk on during the Kavadi festival.

12. Jallikattu is the name of a _____.

DOWN

1. The Lord of Dance.

2. What is mixed with jaggery and milk to make this dish?

4. What is celebrated during Pongal?

6. Natyanjali is the festival of _____.

7. The movie-making world in Tamil Nadu is known as _____.

9. The animals that people try to control during the Jallikattu festival.

10. People give thanks to _____ for giving them a good harvest.

Bricks and stones

Wow! Look, Pushka. The houses are made of mud.

They look really old.

Yes, these are old houses. Now, of course, there are tall buildings in cities. But you will find many houses like these in villages.

MUD AND THATCH

At one time, people built mud and thatch houses. The poor would mix mud and rice husk, while richer people made bricks of mud that they dried in the sun. But all houses used to plaster the walls with lime plaster. This kept insects away, and the white colour reflected sunlight, keeping rooms cool.

TO MEET AND EAT

In the olden days, most large homes would have in their centre a square courtyard with a veranda. This was where the family would sit around and chat, eat meals and meet visitors too. Some houses of wealthier people had many courtyards. Some courtyards would be for the entire family, some only for the women and some that were used just for cooking.

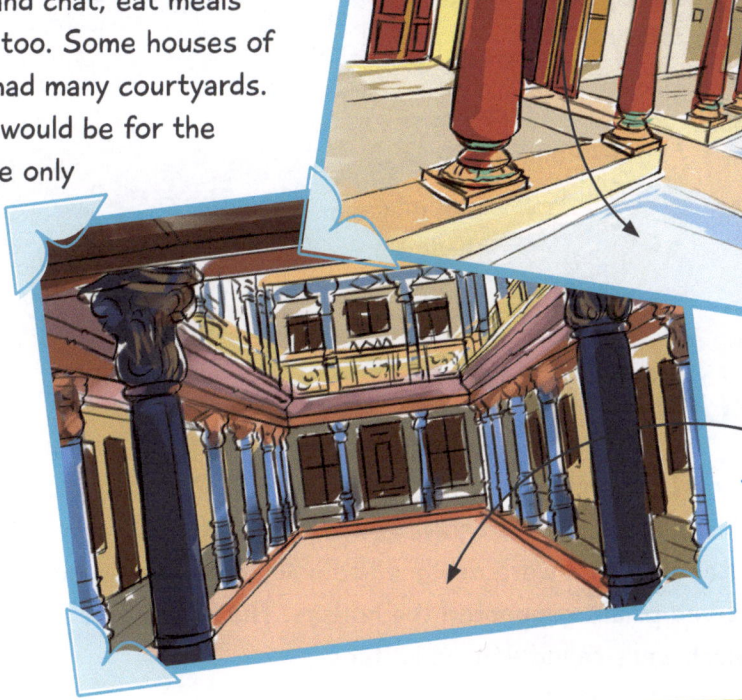

The chatty veranda

The relaxed courtyard

Home sweet home

Draw a house just like the one shown here, and then colour it to look like a mud and thatch house.

Draw here

33

A MUSEUM OF HOUSES

Long ago, different types of people, like weavers, potters, Brahmins and farmers, built homes to suit their professions. Silk weavers' homes were brightly painted and had courtyards, where family members did their weaving. Farmers built houses that gave them space to store their produce.

All these houses can be seen in their original forms at a museum of houses called DakshinaChitra.

ECO-FRIENDLY LIVING

The Chettinad region of Tamil Nadu was inhabited by a lot of wealthy traders and bankers. They built beautiful homes and planned their villages to be really eco-friendly. Walls were made from local materials; roofs were designed to collect rain water, so that it could be reused; beautiful carved pillars supported the houses. These homes also had lovely tiles with detailed designs, which were called Athangudi tiles.

DECORATING THE HOUSE

Tamil Nadu has a lovely tradition of decorating the entrance of houses with a pattern called kolam. People believe that the kolam brings happiness and prosperity to the house. Every morning, before the sun is up, women and girls sweep the floor in front of the house, wash it clean and make lovely, detailed patterns made of rice flour or chalk powder.

TILE STYLE

Mishki wants to paint tiles. Colour in this tile, and help her make it look as nice as the Athangudi tiles of Tamil Nadu.

Standing strong

Oh! Look at those caves! Can we see what's inside?

Yes, we can. Those are the famous Jain caves of Madurai.

CAVES OF MEDITATION

Can you imagine that Jainism has been going strong in Tamil Nadu for over 1000 years? You'll find Jain caves, writings and monasteries that are carved out from the hills. There are twenty-six caves that you can visit. Each cave has a stone bed. Monks used to meditate and live here. Scholars from all over India came here to learn the rules and beliefs of Jainism.

RAMESHWARAM TEMPLE

It is said that Lord Rama prayed at this temple after his victory over Ravana. This temple was once just a small hut. But many kings added on to it. It has a long corridor with nearly 4000 pillars. It is said to be the longest corridor in the world. There is an enormous statue of Nandi, the bull that Lord Shiva rode. It is as tall as the first floor of a building. WOW!

KANYAKUMARI

The city of Kanyakumari has a lovely story. Kanya Devi, an avatar of Goddess Parvati, was to marry Lord Shiva. But the wedding never happened. The rice that was to be made for the wedding remained uncooked. Even now, you can buy stones that look like rice grains, which people believe to be the same uncooked rice.

Did you know?

There are two rocks jutting right into the sea at Kanyakumari. One has an enormous statue of Swami Vivekananda. He was a great Indian philosopher and monk, who, it is said, gained enlightenment while he was meditating here. Imagine how it must have felt to be surrounded by the sea and nothing else.

MEENAKSHI TEMPLE

The Meenakshi Temple in Madurai is one of India's largest temple complexes. The entire temple reflects thousands of years of culture. This huge complex has twelve gateways (called gopurams). One of these is nine storeys tall. It is decorated with detailed carvings of gods, goddesses, gargoyles and griffins; all of these are painted in brilliant colours.

What a riot of colour!

A STORY IN STONE

Near the city of Mahabalipuram, some of the boulders have beautiful carvings on them. These are called The Descent of Ganges. There are carvings of gods, angels, beasts, birds and people, all folding their hands and looking towards a deep cut, which is supposed to be the river Ganga. The story is that millions of years ago, King Bhagiratha brought the Ganga to Earth to seek forgiveness for all his ancestors who had sinned.

Also called Arjuna's Penance, as Arjuna prayed to Lord Shiva here

These are ancient murals on the walls of the durbar hall

ROYAL LIFE

In a place called Thanjavur (also known as Tanjore), there is a beautiful palace. This used to be the capital of the Chola empire. There are many exquisite temples that the kings built. But most incredible is Maratha Palace, with its magnificent halls, corridors, observation towers and courtyards. There is even a museum where we can see how kings and queens dressed, hunted and lived.

Thanjavur is known as the rice bowl of Tamil Nadu because the richest rice fields are found around this area.

A ROCK TEMPLE

The Rock Fort Temple in the city of Tiruchirapalli (called Trichy for short) has three temples. But the highlight is the famous Ucchi Pillayar Temple that you reach after climbing 437 steps. The temple itself is perched on a massive rock that is as tall as twenty-five floors of a building. Wow! We sure will be tired by the time we get there.

ALL SCRAMBLED UP

Pushka has got all these words mixed up. Help him unscramble them to get the right answers. See which clue the word answers. The clues are in a random order. So read them carefully!

- Short for Tiruchirapalli
- Arjuna did this
- There are many of these in the palace
- The one who lives in a palace
- The holy river that came to Earth

G N I K _____

N G A A G _____

H Y T I R C _____

E C N A N E P _____

R O D I R R O C _____

Working hard

Daadu, though this state is so ancient, people seem to use modern equipment. How is that?

You're right. Tamil Nadu has the oldest type of occupation, as well as the most modern. You'll soon see what I mean.

FARMER, FARMER, WHAT DO YOU GROW?

Like a lot of India, farming is an important occupation in Tamil Nadu. The main crop that farmers grow is rice. They also grow millet and pulses. Because the state has a long coastline, coconut trees are in plenty. And, of course, in smaller farms, farmers also grow sugar cane, sunflowers, groundnuts and other smaller crops.

Tea plantation

TIME FOR TEA AND COFFEE

The cool weather of the Nilgiris is perfect for growing coffee and tea. There are beautiful tea and coffee plantations, and lots of people work on these. Many of them work for daily wages. Which means they get paid only on the days that they work. Tough, isn't it?

Coffee plantation

LET'S GO FISHING

With the Bay of Bengal and Indian Ocean lapping Tamil Nadu's shores, there are lots of fisherfolk here. In fact, fishing in the sea, as well as in rivers, is an important occupation. There are more than a million fishermen who depend on fishing and aquaculture. A lot of fish is also exported from Tamil Nadu.

SPINNING A YARN

Another very important industry in Tamil Nadu is the textile business. Can you believe that almost half of India's yarn is spun in Tamil Nadu?

MAKING CARS

Many, many cars and car parts that are made in India are manufactured in Tamil Nadu. Indian and international carmakers have their factories here.

GIANTS IN TECHNOLOGY

People in Tamil Nadu love education. There are plenty of engineers here. And so, of course, the computer industry is huge too! Millions of people work in the computer industry—as engineers, coders, designers, animators. It's definitely very modern here!

BIG INDUSTRY

There are many other major industries as well. Leather, sugar, paper, telecom—these are just a few businesses where many large companies have factories and employ thousands of people.

GEARING UP

Pushka loves factories. He has found some gears and is trying to count the circles in these gears. Can you help him?

Yum yum yum

Aah! My favourite part. Daadu, what's that soft, round, yummy looking thing? Everyone seems to be eating it.

Those are idlis— Tamil Nadu's most famous food.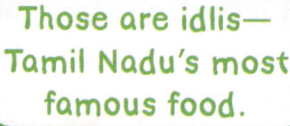

IDLIS AND DOSAS

Idlis and dosas are eaten very often in Tamil Nadu— whether it's for breakfast, lunch, or dinner. Made of rice and pulses, idlis are soft and springy. Dosas are crispy pancakes made from the same batter. There are many version of dosas. Uttappam, appam and neer dosa are just a few.

ON A LEAF

In the olden days, Tamilians, like a lot of people in other parts of India, used banana leaves as plates. Even now, in some villages and during weddings and festivals, people serve food on banana leaves.
How eco-friendly!

FROM CHETTINAD WITH LOVE

The food made in an area called Chettinad is different from the food in the rest of Tamil Nadu. It is very spicy and has lots of non-vegetarian dishes that use chicken, lamb, crab and fish.

RICE IS NICE

Tamilians just LOVE rice, and they eat it in different ways. They mix it with a curry called sambar. They also mix it with curd. Oooh! It's all so delicious. They make lots of things with rice.

Tamarind rice

Lemon rice

The desserts of Tamil Nadu are famous too! There are dozens of them, but here are some of the most famous ones.

Payasam is a yummy dish made of rice and milk.

Chakkarai pongal is a porridge of rice, lentils, jaggery and milk.

Nei poli is a sweet roti made of lentils, jaggery and flour

MULLIGATAWNY SOUP

When the British came to Tamil Nadu, they liked the taste of food. But they modified it. Based on Tamil spices, a soup called mulligatawny was created. The name comes from the Tamil words millagu and thanni. 'Millagu' means pepper and 'thanni' means water.

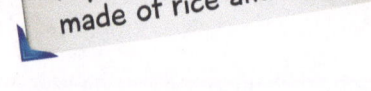

SNACK TIME

MURUKKU

These are crunchy circles that are spicy and salty. They are a teatime snack.

MEDU VADA

Oooh! This is a partner of idli. It's a soft but crisp doughnut shaped dish.

Hey, wait! We can't leave just yet. I have to have some of Tamil Nadu's famous kaapi. That's another way of saying coffee.

The filter coffee here is very famous. It is served in two small steel cups. It's very hot, so people cool it by pouring it from one cup into the other.

TASTY GRID

There are ten yummy dishes from Tamil Nadu hidden in this word grid. Pushka wants to find and eat them all. Can you find them before he does?

D	O	S	A	E	D	C	V	B	A
V	N	K	M	U	R	U	K	K	U
Q	W	E	T	Y	U	I	O	N	M
U	T	T	A	P	P	A	M	E	E
P	U	S	Q	S	Q	J	H	E	D
O	P	A	Y	A	S	A	M	R	U
N	G	B	Y	D	E	P	H	D	V
G	E	T	R	D	F	P	H	O	A
A	W	D	W	D	S	A	H	S	D
L	F	I	D	L	I	M	G	A	A

What to wear?

What lovely colours these ladies are wearing! What are they, Daadu?

They are Kanjeevaram saris made from special silk.

SILK OF THE GODS

Kanjeevaram silk is very famous here, and women love to wear these saris on special occasions. People believe that the weavers of this kind of silk have descended from the master weavers who wove for the gods. Whether that is true or not, the fact is that these weavers weave the most beautiful silk using mulberry silk thread. They are then turned into gorgeous saris.

Kanjeevaram sari

ANGAVASTRA

This is a long cloth, sometimes with a pattern, which men throw around their shoulders.

LUNGI STYLE

The traditional clothing for men in Tamil Nadu is the veshti—a long, rectangular cloth (like a lungi) that they drape around themselves like sarongs. Veshtis used to be worn with angavastras, but now men wear them with shirts.

Dress Up

Pushka has decided to wear a veshti. He wants to wear it exactly like the man in the picture. Can you draw it on Pushka and colour it?

Autograph, please?

Everybody seems to know them.

Who are all these people, Daadu?

Tamil Nadu has many, many world-famous people. Come, let's meet some of them.

C.V. RAMAN

He won the Nobel Prize in Physics almost ninety years ago.

A.P.J. ABDUL KALAM

The much-loved scientist and once the President of India; he was popular with both children and adults.

SRINIVASA RAMANUJAN

He was one of the world's greatest mathematicians. He developed important concepts in maths.

M.S. SUBBULAKSHMI

She was a classical singer who was so good that a stamp was released in her name.

R.K. LAXMAN

He was a famous cartoonist. He created the famous Common Man, and he drew many cartoons about society. He won the Padma Bhushan, as well as the Padma Vibhushan.

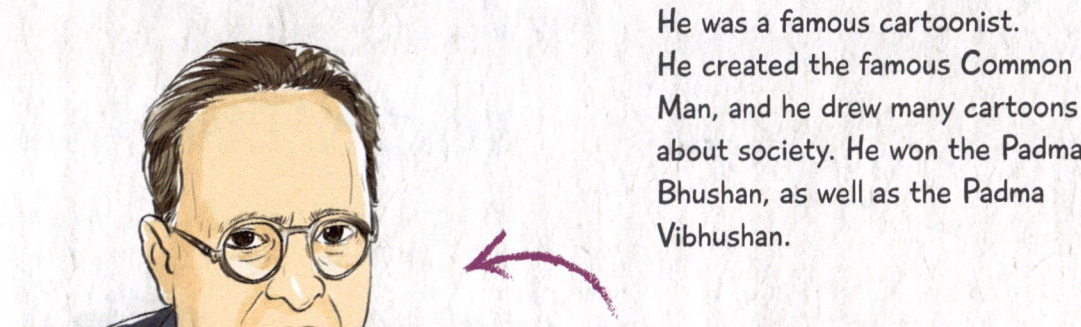

R.K. NARAYAN

He was R.K. Laxman's brother. He was a famous author who wrote lovely stories called *Malgudi Days*, which were about life in a Tamil village. He also wrote many other books. He too won the Padma Vibhushan.

THE AMRITRAJ BROTHERS

Vijay, Anand and Ashok—all of whom became international tennis stars.

> Did you know?
> 5 September is celebrated as Teachers' Day because it is Dr Radhakrishnan's birthday.

VISWANATHAN ANAND

He was a World Chess Champion and the first Indian to win the title of Grandmaster.

DR SARVEPALLI RADHAKRISHNAN

He was India's second president.

RAJINIKANTH

Though he was born in Karnataka to a Maratha family, this famous actor is so popular in Tamil Nadu that people collect in their thousands to see him. When his movies are released, fans queue all night long to make it to the first screening.

A.R. RAHMAN

He is a music composer and singer who has composed for hundreds of films. He has even won an Oscar, which is an American award for doing terrific work in cinema.

REKHA

She is a famous actor who is the daughter of yet another famous actor, Gemini Ganesan.

M.G. RAMACHANDRAN

He was an actor who became a politician and was chief minister of Tamil Nadu for many years. He too was so popular that his posters and cutouts were plastered all over Tamil Nadu.

WHICH ONE IS DIFFERENT?

From the names given below, one is different. Which one and why?

A.R. Rahman   Rekha   Rajinikanth   R.K. Narayan

C.V. Raman   Srinivasa Ramanujan   A.P.J. Abdul Kalam   R.K. Laxman

Dr Radhakrishnan   A.P.J. Abdul Kalam   M.G. Ramachandran   C.V. Raman

Anand Amritraj   Vijay Amritraj   Viswanathan Anand   Rajinikanth

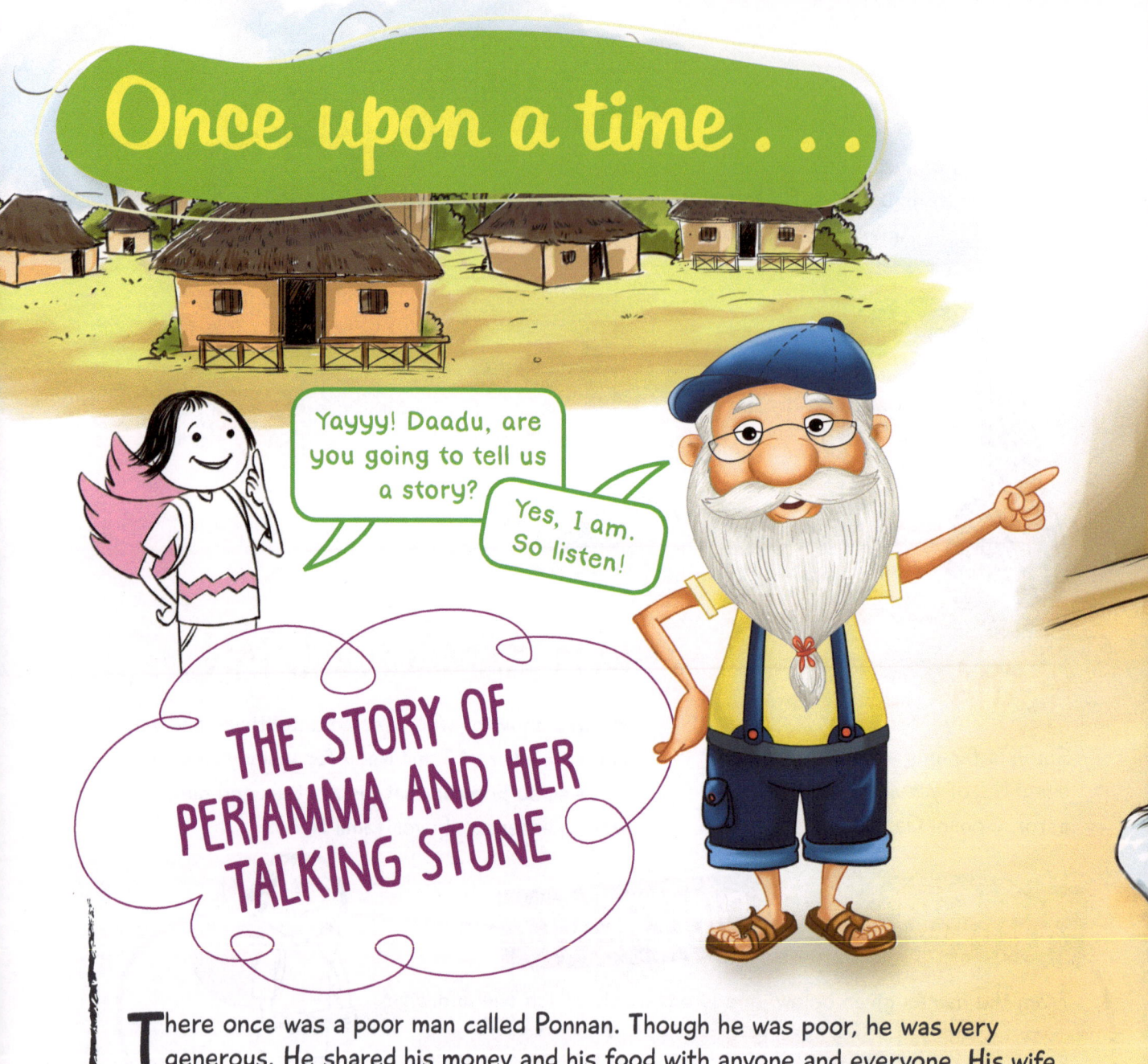

Yayyy! Daadu, are you going to tell us a story?

Yes, I am. So listen!

THE STORY OF PERIAMMA AND HER TALKING STONE

There once was a poor man called Ponnan. Though he was poor, he was very generous. He shared his money and his food with anyone and everyone. His wife, Periamma, would get very angry with him.

'We have so little ourselves,' she would scold him. 'How can we afford to feed people? Stop bringing people home to eat with us. I will not serve anyone any food.'

But Ponnan just could not help it. Whenever he saw anyone hungry, he would invite them home. Soon, everyone in the village knew that if they needed a meal, they could just go to Ponnan's house. They all took advantage of sweet, generous Ponnan. Poor Periamma was at her wits' end.

'I must come up with an idea to stop him from doing this,' she thought to herself.

The next day, as usual, Ponnan brought three people with him for lunch.

'I could not help it,' he explained to Periamma. 'They were so hungry.'

'If they are hungry, they can eat your food,' snapped Periamma. 'I have no more to give them.'

But Ponnan was so generous that he gave all his food to his guests and stayed hungry himself. Periamma thought that if she continued doing this, he would change his ways. But he didn't.

Over the weeks, Ponnan became thinner and thinner, while the villagers shamelessly came to his home and ate his portion of food. Finally, Periamma could bear it no longer.

'If I can't change Ponnan, I will have to teach the villagers a lesson,' she decided.

As expected, the next day too, Ponnan arrived for lunch with two of the same men who had come the previous day. This time, Periamma was ready. She had decorated the stone with which she ground coconut paste. She had put a garland of flowers around it and added a vermilion tikka. She sat in front of the stone as if in deep prayer.

'Why are you praying to a cooking stone?' the two villagers said, laughing at her.

'Oh, you have come,' she said. 'Last night, I had a dream that this stone would come to life and hit on the head the next person who ate food in this house. And you know how Ponnan is. He will not eat until his guests have eaten. I don't want our guests to be harmed. So I am praying to this stone.'

The men stared. They realized that if they ate first, the stone would hurt them.

'Ponnan, I think you had better eat first,' they said slyly. Poor Ponnan didn't understand what was going on. So he ate the food. When it was finished, Periamma turned to the men. 'I am so sorry, there is no more food left for you.'

The men understood her trick. And from that day onwards, no one came to eat at Ponnan's house.

TRAVEL DIARY

Have you enjoyed this trip to Tamil Nadu with your friends Mishki and Pushka—and, of course, with Daadu Dolma?

Now you can make your own Tamil Nadu diary. And if you ever visit Tamil Nadu, make sure you take pictures and put them in the photo box.

The first place I would visit in Tamil Nadu:

_____

If I ever meet Rajinikanth, this is what I would say to him:

_____

The one dish I am definitely going to eat:

_____

The monument that I find the most interesting:

_____

The one famous person from Tamil Nadu that I would love to meet:

_____

If I were Tamil, my name would be:

_____

The festival from Tamil Nadu that I think would be the most fun:

_____

The five words that I feel describe Tamil Nadu the best are:

_____

_____

_____

_____

My Tamil Nadu memories:

ANSWERS

page 9 RHYME TIME

dice, lice, mice, nice, spice, vice

page 11 CROP SHOP

S	U	G	A	R	C	A	N	E
J	L	R	F	I	O	T	E	A
R	J	O	P	C	F	Z	D	B
Y	F	U	E	E	F	G	C	V
P	X	N	F	G	E	W	E	H
Y	W	D	Q	W	E	T	C	W
B	A	N	A	N	A	P	V	A
R	P	U	W	S	E	D	F	Z
G	W	T	C	W	D	U	T	G
C	O	C	O	N	U	T	S	M

page 13 SPOT THEM ALL

page 16 WHAT'S ODD

Mall, Chennai, Portuguese

page 19 CRACK THE CODE

WE WANT TO BE FREE

page 21 MATCH THE WORDS

Hi—Vanakkam; Sorry—Mannikkanum; Happy birthday!—Pirandha naal vazhthukkal!; Good night!—Iravu vanakkam; You!—Neenga!; What's your name?— Unga pérenna?

page 31 CROSSWORD TIME

Across/Down answers:
MEENAKSHI, NATARAJA, RICE, RED, DANCE, HARVEST, KOLLYWOOD, PONGAL, BULL, NATURE, COALS, SPORT

page 39 ALL SCRAMBLED UP

King, Ganga, Trichy, penance, corridor

page 43 GEARING UP

18 circles

page 47 TASTY GRID

D	O	S	A	E	D	C	V	B	A
V	N	K	M	U	R	U	K	K	U
Q	W	E	T	Y	U	I	O	N	M
U	T	T	A	P	P	A	M	E	E
P	U	S	Q	S	Q	J	H	E	D
O	P	A	Y	A	S	A	M	R	U
N	G	B	Y	D	E	P	H	D	V
G	E	T	R	D	F	P	H	O	A
A	W	D	W	D	S	A	H	S	D
L	F	I	D	L	I	M	G	A	A

page 53 WHICH ONE IS DIFFERENT?

R.K. Narayan, R.K. Laxman, C.V. Raman, Rajinikanth